FRANÇOIS CATROUX

TEXT BY DAVID NETTO

FOREWORD BY DIANE VON FURSTENBERG

DESIGN BY TAKAAKI MATSUMOTO

FRANÇOIS CATROUX

RIZZOLI
NEW YORK

New York · Paris · London · Milan

I can never thank
François enough for
making our life
so beautiful in every way

Betty

TABLE OF CONTENTS

François Catroux's impressive body of work speaks for itself. Palaces, houses, boats, planes—his incredible talent has created magic all around the world, and established him as a guru of taste.

Born in Mascara to a prestigious French military family, he left for Paris as early as he could while never forgetting the colonial atmosphere and elegance—the colors, the sensuality—of his native birthplace, Algeria.

François knows how to create disciplined grandeur and majestic architecture while combining them with incomparable comfort; he knows how to achieve both scale and coziness at the same time. This "grand coziness" is something all his own.

His first big job—the Milan palace of couturiere Mila Schön—was a triumph, and his marriage to Paris "It" girl Betty Saint the same year projected him on the covers of prestigious magazines and declared him the upcoming most talented interior architect. I met François at about that time, at a dinner party in his astonishing apartment on the Quai de Béthune. I was curious to see that very talked-about modern apartment, which had been photographed by Horst in the pages of American *Vogue*. Yellow and white, bare and sleek, it looked like an abstract painting of the time . . . a Vasarely, or an Albers maybe?

We became very close friends over the next decades, so it was obvious when in 1985 I decided to spend more time in Paris that I would ask him to help me with the beautiful apartment I had found on the rue de Seine. I was at the time very involved in publishing and would entertain writers there—so I wanted something chic, but not pretentious. I brought my pre-Raphaelite paintings from my apartment in New York, bought a few turn of the century pieces in Italy, and François created a most wonderful bohemian-chic décor. Twenty years later and a few houses away on the same rue de Seine he made me another striking apartment, one that corresponds better with my "seldom in Paris" life of efficient business trips.

It was therefore clear that I would call on him when my husband decided to build *Eos*, our floating home—a ninety-three-meter, three-masted motorsailer—or to redo our house in Beverly Hills. The boat where we now spend four months a year is perfection. Every detail is refined and functional, elegant *and* practical. And our Frank Lloyd Wright-inspired house is original and totally cozy!

To live in a Catroux interior makes you forever thankful, for François listens to his clients' needs and dreams, and he delivers not only tasteful chic, but glorious comfort.

Diane von Furstenberg
Aboard *Eos*, August 2015

If you had ventured out to dinner one night in Paris during the early 1970s—a rather fearless and magical time for style anywhere, but perhaps in Paris more than anyplace else—you might have come upon a singular group. If it was a Sunday you would usually have found them in a Chinese restaurant, where ten or more could easily be seated and their preference indulged for a round table. Boisterous and glittering, they would be easy to notice, for this was the entourage surrounding Yves Saint Laurent. Besides the designer, many of the faces in his company would also have been familiar, and some are even more so now. For while Saint Laurent and his muse Loulou de la Falaise have both gone and passed into fashion myth too soon, YSL's partner Pierre Bergé and his confidante and inspirational source Betty Catroux (same surname is not a coincidence—she is married to our subject) live in the Paris of today as legends to those who care about style and its history. The era and its characters have been discussed and described endlessly, though perhaps most memorably by Alicia Drake in her book *The Beautiful Fall*, and inspired a thousand young designers' mood boards. Lately there have also come two Saint Laurent movies. In fact, there have been books written about the lives and careers and loves and taste and cultural contributions of nearly everybody at this table, save one: the handsome fellow at the back—on the left behind Loulou with longish brown hair—not as loud or personally expressive as the others but just as much of a presence . . . This is the decorator François Catroux.

Fashion as usual claims the lion's share of public attention, and such is the fate of interior design when held up for examination next to its more famous cousin that recognition in the form of a book should come late. But François Catroux, husband of the legendary Betty, childhood schoolmate of YSL in Algeria, and close friend of his and Bergé's in adulthood, has been an innovator and interpreter of French style in decoration on the international scene for nearly five decades. He began his career as a very committed modernist, but the style in which he works has evolved with the passage of time and context. It is difficult to say if Catroux's evolution as a designer has been driven by personal inspirations or by reaction to a changing zeitgeist; in decoration the truth is usually a little of both. What is even more difficult to say is whether the primary genius of François Catroux lies in the occasions when he has broken new ground—which are specific, if not prolific—or in his body of work in the aggregate, which is colossal.

To anybody interested in design, the question invites careful examination. Many interiors by François Catroux may at first appear to represent refinements upon preexisting aesthetic styles, rather than the invention of new ones. But to perceive Catroux's body of work as valuing commitment to grace over the breaking of new ground is to invite the danger of mistakenly thinking, to paraphrase Tallulah, that "there is less here than meets the eye."

François and Betty Catroux have set the standard for leading a fashionable life. A selection of private views of this dazzling couple and their circle through the years, with close friends Yves Saint Laurent, Loulou de la Falaise, Mrs. William S. Paley, Pierre Bergé, and Diane von Furstenburg

In the first place, more than almost any other decorator, Catroux has deliberately and serially rejected the idea of working in a single style. The briefest flip through this book will confirm the *scope* of what is already well known, that he has worked successfully in many styles over six decades. Secondly, as a designer Catroux prizes a flexible approach and successful results over novelty for its own sake. He is capable in his work of subjugating his own voice in favor of telling a story—as long as he feels it is the "right" story—and in favor of taking the strongest possible position relative to context. He is eclectic but never random. He defines himself as an interior architect rather than a decorator, and his instinct for architecture is the part of his talent he values most ("It comes before decoration—and only a few people notice it except some real pros"). He is, to use an architectural term, site-specific in his approach. He is also a decorator whose work has consistently been "of its time," evolving. Not so much a signature style—not at all, actually—as a signature sense of refinement embedded *within* multiple styles, from Mod to Neoclassical to Postmodern to other things not seen before, always responsive to architecture and to place.

But is it French? And is the work of François Catroux ever *really* traditional, even when it pretends to be?

Catroux is embarrassed by too much talk about method—like Fred Astaire, he has a strong work ethic and makes things look easier than they are. In his time Fred Astaire was not thought of the same way as Nijinsky, but with the passage of years he is now correctly understood to be every inch an artist. However, being recognized for originality where it is rightly his due is important to François Catroux, as was demonstrated early in our first interview. He opened the conversation by making one point emphatically: "I never copied anybody." A claim many designers are fond of making with predictably varying degrees of veracity, but in Catroux's case it seems to be truer than most. Also true, and perhaps the most surprising aspect about the story of his career is that he never went to school for design and never trained professionally with any other decorator. He is entirely self-taught, one of the more compelling aspects of this remarkable story.

Obviously, there have been influences. But where—and from whom—did he learn the art of composition and flair? At home with his family? Not so much, apparently. "My parents had terrible taste, ghastly houses," he recalls with some humor today. "Everything was fake Louis XVI. I was already a decorator when I was five years old."

ORAN, 1949

Home and family was in French Colonial Algeria, where he likely acquired a love of and instinct for using organic materials—wicker, straw, matchstick blinds—that pervades even his quite grand interiors, giving them a light touch and feeling, however subtle, of the exotic. Catroux's family were landowners and colonialists; wealthy but not specifically of aristocratic lineage, what he describes as "*grands bourgeois.*" His grandfather was the famous French general Georges Catroux. His grandmother

Marie was a Spanish heiress and the owner of properties managed for the family by her son, Catroux's father André. Among these was a vineyard in Mascara, the small city in the northwestern region of the country known for leather goods, olive oil, and especially wine (the etymology of the English word for cosmetics is unrelated). The wine produced by Catroux's family was eponymously titled Le Mascara. It was the sunset of French colonial rule in North Africa; not the violent years, but the beginning of the end. The long-simmering colonial tensions of France and Algeria were to come to a head in earnest in 1954, and for most of Catroux's early childhood the world's attention was consumed by World War II.

It was a romantic and moody place to be a young person, full of contrasts—of whitewashed classical architecture in the French area of the small city, and wildness, the wildness of the north African landscape, of white stucco and red earth. Catroux recalls impressions of beauty and starkness simultaneously. "I remember the deserted naked mountains around my native Mascara, which seemed to come right up with no transition to the beautiful irrigated flat fields where the vineyards were growing. Also the smell of roses and eucalyptus. And the heat. An unbearable heat, lasting for months."

At the age of twelve, Catroux left home and family in Mascara to go to boarding school in Oran. It was here, in a remarkable prelude to the time in Paris twenty years later, that as classmates in the same school he met the young Yves Saint Laurent. "Yves and I were exactly the same age, maybe twelve. He was a day student and I a boarder at Sacre Coeur. He was always very well-dressed, with a tie and jacket and we the boarders wore a black uniform with no collar, like a Chinese jacket." Catroux was witness to the merciless teasing Saint Laurent endured as a youth, which contributed much to the formation of his well-known tormented personality. "I saw how he was picked on by the other kids. I wanted to protect him, and offered him friendship—but he refused." Not merely delicate, from early youth Saint Laurent's sexuality was impossible to hide. "After that time at school we didn't see each other for seven years, until Paris when Yves was at Dior."

It was in Paris in the very early 1960s that François Catroux and Yves Saint Laurent met again through Vogue art director Alexander Lieberman, but it was through their mutual attachment to Betty that they later became so close ("I was quite clever managing my husband and Yves," Betty has said playfully). Enter this into evidence of the strange power of creative types to manage and compartmentalize painful experiences: during the nearly fifty years of intimate association and the friendship that followed—each at the top of their fields, each closely bonded to the same woman, each facing the other across the table night after night at dinner with the same entourage—the two designers never once discussed the trauma of Saint Laurent's upbringing in Oran to which Catroux had been such a close witness. Never? "*Never*," Catroux confirms today, saying much by saying so little. "Yves and I never spoke about our early days at school."

As a prelude to the discussion of François Catroux's career, let me point out that when he left Algeria as a young man he did go to Paris—but following the required service of two years in the French army, very soon after that to New York. Like his long-suffering schoolmate who also made his way from Algeria to Paris as soon as he could (but never left), Catroux had waited all his early life to get out of the colonies and into the capital. Why then decamp almost immediately for New York? Was Paris the capital of fashion at that time, but not of all categories of design?

Upon closer investigation, perhaps not. Evidence of a transatlantic exchange of ideas between French and American decorators after World War II can be obscure, but the son of Billy Baldwin's business partner Edward Martin Jr. (the famous interior design firm was actually known as Baldwin & Martin) tells a story that gives a clue as to what the Old World thought about the New, and specifically the high regard in which the French held the work of Mr. Baldwin. On a youthful trip to France in the mid-1970s, Brian Martin went to call on his father's friend, the spectacularly aged Madeleine Castaing. Champagne was served and champagne was drunk, and at the end of the visit Mme. Castaing was clearly moved by her meeting with the good-looking boy in his early twenties. She grabbed him by the shoulders and said with great emotion: "We all copied things, all of us. But Billy and your father—*never* did." A kiss on the young man's mouth both underscored and ended this confession.

NEW YORK CITY, 1960

Perhaps at exactly the same age as the boy in the Paris story, the young François Catroux was living in New York and working as a location scout for *Elle* magazine. After a stint in the army, he had arrived armed with a raft of high-level introductions from Marguerite, his step-grandmother and the second wife of general Georges Catroux (a cousin of Jean Cocteau, she had taken François to see *La Belle et La Bête* when he was twelve). Catroux recalls that her domineering personality had also earned her the nickname "Queen Margot." One of the first places he went in New York was Billy Baldwin's famous studio apartment at 166 East 61st Street, and he describes with total recall the electrifying impact of that visit today: "That was the chicest apartment I had seen until that time. Because then, you see, only the Americans knew how achieve that combination of French style and American modernism. With English comfort." This may sound surprising, given that we are used to thinking of France as the epicenter of chic in all things, but French decorating around 1960 (as exemplified by Jansen and Henri Samuel) was highly and almost exclusively classical. During this period Catroux also visited the New York apartments of Cole Porter at the Waldorf Towers and Kitty Miller at 550 Park Avenue (both also done by Baldwin), the latter famously containing Goya's *Red Boy* over the living room sofa. And in a different, more modernist vein, that of the philanthropist Mary Lasker.

But after Baldwin's, the American house that fascinated him most was in New Canaan, Connecticut: the home of architect Philip Johnson. Catroux went to see Johnson at his famous Glass House several times.

These recollections make clear how Catroux's training as a decorator was acquired. It was not by the more usual formal instruction or work in a design studio, but by using his eyes—and the place that opened them was America. Modernism was waiting there to meet the French boy who had grown up in the colonies surrounded by fake Louis XVI furniture, and with it visual lessons in the potential of architecture and decoration to be fused into something powerfully new. In New York, the young Catroux encountered environments that had been designed with equal success but using the two disparate methods of innovation and refinement. Seeing these provided the formative experiences that in a design office might have otherwise been limited to an individual voice or single point of view. Instead, Catroux found things to appreciate in the originality of Baldwin's apartment and the purity of the Glass House—one a free form composition, the other a manifesto—and he understood that the philosophies driving either project could become an eloquent voice in design. In short, before he even became a designer, the New World made him a flexible thinker.

It is a curious twist that in this case the decorator was the "innovator" (Billy Baldwin was an undisputed original, and the older he got the truer this became), and the world-famous modernist architect actually the "refiner" (Johnson always insisted he was not a form-giver; the Glass House is a distillation of ideas actually invented by Johnson's mentor Mies van der Rohe). But the visits to the Baldwin apartment and the Glass House did lead to an appreciation for the dual methods behind their conception, and equal respect for their successful results. In fifty years of work in his own career Catroux has been a proponent of both, switching with indifference from being an innovator to a refiner, as happy to be one as the other

So while he may have been a decorator instinctively at the age of five, it is also clear that what Catroux saw in New York at the time of his stay in 1960 was the beginning of his training as one. This education by osmosis occurred not in school, not in a design office, but exclusively through experiences "in the field," impressions that were forged when Catroux was in his early twenties. This is nearly a decade before the start of his career in 1967, but in them lie the beginnings of his diversity and range as a decorator—qualities in which he may well be in a class by himself.

One of Catroux's most loyal clients and admirers, a close collaborator with whom he has done several houses, has pointed out that it might be more accurate to call him a European decorator rather than a French one. This is because his interiors have been conceived and executed using contemporary furniture, English antiques, Art Deco, and in the amalgam of taste and periods that defies succinct definition but is known as the "Style Rothschild." What is certain is that the work of his early career begins with a jolt, not in France or even in Europe—but in a real-life version of Stanley Kubrick's *2001: A Space Odyssey*, with the radical modernism of the Mila Schön atelier in Milan.

François Catroux's first major commission came to him by chance introduction, or at least was set up to appear so. At the Rue du Bac apartment of Knoll International president Yves Vidal he was presented to Mila Schön, a then-prominent Italian fashion designer visiting Paris. Something clicked over drinks, and at the end of their meeting she turned to the young man, just turned thirty and with no relevant work experience, and asked if he would be interested in working for her on a special project—the design of her new showroom in Milan. Vidal and Catroux were close, and the Knoll executive regarded Catroux as something of a protégé. It is likely he set up the meeting expecting it to end favorably, and when it did he offered the support of the Knoll offices in Milan for execution. "I locked myself in a hotel room working furiously for three months," Catroux recalls today. As an atelier the hotel room proved adequate; with Knoll's organizational and infrastructural support the project was completed smoothly and successfully, though the latter term may be an understatement. The Mila Schön showroom was a futuristic, minimalistic, theater-in-the-round for fashion—exactly right for the times, delivered by an ingénue, and it caused a sensation in the design world. Catroux's work, his first project, landed him on the January 1968 cover of the prestigious French arts journal *L'Oeil* (opposite page).

Apartments followed for the director of Christian Dior in Paris and a prominent publisher on Fifth Avenue in New York City, both published in *L'Oeil* (pp. 44–45) and in *Vogue* (pp. 46–50) respectively. The latter was photographed by Horst, who soon after also shot François and Betty's own apartment on the Quai de Béthune (pp. 38–43)—which then also appeared in *Vogue*—making the years 1967–71 for François Catroux about as big a public opening as any decorator has ever had. At the same time as this explosion of publicity for his work as a designer, Betty's singular beauty and visibility (and to be perfectly candid, her notoriety) as YSL's female alter ego and ambassador of his style to the world was also growing. Betty has rather perfectly described herself "*une femme antibourgeoise*," but she and François were married in great style in Cap Ferrat in 1967 and soon after started a family. Betty, who loves dancing and making statements for dramatic effect in equal measure, has often said that she met the two most important men in her life in a nightclub. While this statement referring to her husband and the man who called her his female twin happens to be true (and we know the nightclub was Regine's), a version told sometimes by François has them meeting at an art opening, which was in any case the first time François saw her, and he is unsure today if they actually spoke. But I prefer the lady's story, in which history is made on the dance floor and at night, don't you?

While François Catroux's level of talent as a designer was recognized immediately, being married to one of the most stylish women in the world and one of the great muses of fashion there has ever been did not fail to add to the velocity of his early and sudden success. Being part of the Saint Laurent set in Paris (rather than at a Catholic boarding school in Oran) put him in the right place at the right time, as did the couple's very heady social life in general—for which, as any decorator knows, there is no substitute as a means of attracting clients.

Opening Act: the Mila Schön atelier in Milan makes fashion shows into theater in the round, the January 1968 cover of *L'Oeil*— and a career.

"Decadence!" an amused Catroux recalls today of the Paris apartment he designed for his mother-in-law. The pairing of eighteenth-century objects and modern architecture was not a first, but when it ended up on the cover of the 1973 *Connaissance des Arts* book *Décoration* it became one of the most influential examples of this gesture.

While the modernism of these early projects is generally related to the aesthetics of Stanley Kubrick, NASA, and David Hicks (in other words they are au courant, but part of a narrative that by the end of the 1960s was already freely flowing), they also contain significant moments of design innovation. To explore this claim, let's get specific and identify one distinct Catroux invention of this era: the unadorned and minimalist stainless steel chimneypiece.

This dramatic and much-copied device first appears at his and Betty's own Quai de Béthune apartment on the Île Saint-Louis. He uses it again at the 1969 Paris apartment published in *L'Oeil*, and shortly after that in another Paris apartment of that time for Betty's mother. Here it is augmented provocatively with an eighteenth-century ormolu and bronze rhinoceros clock, one of the ultimate examples of an object in the French high Rococo style of the 1740s. It was this third version that became the best-known, when an image of the modern fireplace and its shocking period ornament was featured on the cover of the 1973 *Connaissance des Arts* book *Decoration* (opposite page). The steel mantel-and-clock pairing, which came about because the designer was not working from scratch but with a collection of eighteenth-century objects and furniture his mother-in-law wished to retain, foreshadows the interest Catroux would soon develop in combining the architecture of the Now with seventeenth-and eighteenth-century antiques. A conversation begins with this room between modernism and the past which Catroux has yet to abandon.

That well-conceived architecture has the power to endure, even as styles of decoration may change, is a conviction Catroux has maintained in all periods of his work. The steel mantel in Catroux's own Quai de Béthune apartment survived the redesign of 1976, during which the designer transformed this space from a 'Mod' environment into its second phase: a contemporary investigation of the ideas encountered at his meeting with Billy Baldwin in New York fifteen years before (p. 20). The living room of the redone apartment is full of matchstick blinds used both as shades and room dividers, white tailored sofas with batik pillows, and wicker. In the bedroom there is now the drama of a coromandel lacquer screen (one of which Baldwin's apartment also contained). Yet the steel fireplace remains, and in doing so checks two boxes rare enough in decoration: it is not only a signature Catroux innovation circa 1970, but also a survivor into subsequent, less radical eras in which Catroux begins to let go of sleekness in favor of the exotic.

In this designer's hands modernism becomes something more intimate and humanistic than extreme. It is blended with the suggestions (some obvious and others less so) of other cultures—in this case Asian. He also finds new ways to blur the difference between architecture and decoration, dividing the living room from the entrance with a scrimlike partition of matchstick blinds. This is not quite a wall and certainly not a shade, yet is made of the same material that hangs both on the walls and in the windows. Look closely and you will notice a subtle hierarchy at work: where the matchstick material covers the walls, in fact acting *as* one in the middle of the room, it is edged with black tape; at the windows it is untrimmed. On the entrance side of the living room, the floating matchstick blind "wall" serves as a backdrop for a steel and glass console of Catroux's own design, while a white upholstered sofa backs up to it on the sitting room side. The white upholstery, batik pillows, and round wicker tables are very much manifestations of the Billy Baldwin style, transatlantic echoes of the visit to New York ten years before.

The 1976 redecoration of Quai de Béthune spelled an end—for a time—to Catroux's Mod beginnings as a designer, and the start of something which has characterized the rest of his career: the pursuit of an aesthetic richer than straightforward modernism, of a style at once both old and new. It is an investigation he has never since abandoned.

This version of the Quai de Béthune apartment is also one of his most exotic projects. Here the leftover futurism of the first scheme (elements like the steel mantel) collides with the classicism and patina of objects newly introduced to the space—things like the colossal Atlas figure supporting an armillary sphere at left of the fireplace, and the lacquer screen over the bed. More than a few of these items have followed Catroux from house to house through the years and are still owned by him presently, found today in the apartment he and Betty share on the Rue de Lille (follow the black-and-white disc which appears to be Asian but is in fact by Jean Dunand as it migrates down from the fireplace wall to become a tabletop).

Among the potential clients who noticed this change in philosophy from Kubrick to—well, something else—and whose curiosity was peaked by it were prominent members of the French branch of the Rothschild family. A couple whose name as patrons of design, architecture, and collecting needs no introduction, they decided around that time that Catroux was ready for them.

SEINE ET MARNE, 1975

The taste of the banking dynasty, developed throughout Europe over a hundred years of residences that outshone many royal seats in splendor, is so well known as to have earned its own sobriquet: *le style Rothschild*. Commissions for the Rothschilds have proved to be a watershed career moment for many decorators, for reasons both obvious and unsurprising. To name a few: the resources are limitless, not just in financial terms but in the form of furniture and art just waiting in the wings to be used. As clients they are highly enlightened and experienced in their taste; they know what they want and provide a strong direction with family collections to draw from. For a certain social milieu, they *set* the style (despite Catroux's insistence today that "it's the opposite of my style, the Rothschild style."). What this client wanted when she and her husband decided in 1975 to build a lodge on the grounds of the massive nineteenth-century chateau of Ferrières was a modern, intimate house. Modern on the outside, that is, but with an interior that looked like a proper residence in the Rothschild tradition.

There were significant challenges associated with this project, both for client and designer. The wife was a woman not lacking in boldness or self-esteem, and she must have prided herself on her sure instinct for patronage in choosing to work with a decorator whose taste had gone in less than ten years—or was about to—from the idiom of the Mila Schön atelier to working now in a deeply historical vein. Catroux

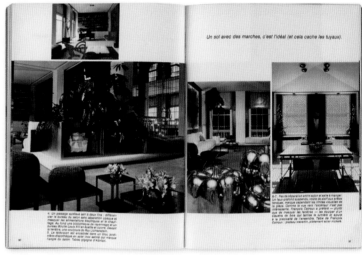

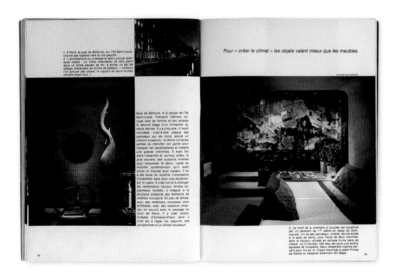

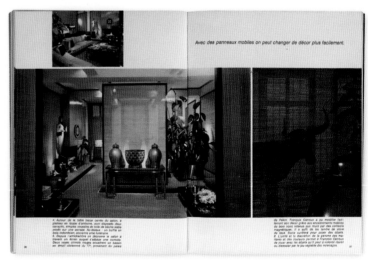

In a London apartment of 1973 Catroux explores his interest in shaping space by using platforms, different levels, and minimal furniture. His own Quai de Béthune apartment, in its second iteration, was a step away from that towards the use of sensual and exotic materials.

Asian and exotic influences take the Quai de Béthune apartment away from its Mod origins and into the 1970's, in pursuit of something richer than orthodox modernism. Antiques appear, including an Atlas that was a gift from Hélène Rochas. The steel mantel, however, remains.

was being entrusted to do so by a woman who took her stewardship of the family aesthetic very seriously—perhaps more seriously than anyone actually born to the name. Other decorators tapped by the family such as Henri Samuel (and later Geoffrey Bennison) had been working in an opulent vocabulary for years—they possessed and had already previously cultivated established reputations as palatial decorators. Catroux had no such reputation—in fact quite the opposite, as we have seen: he was at this point in his career the epitome of Hip.

But the bet paid off, and the success of his work at Ferrières ushered in what can be termed Catroux's "middle period," in which he began, around 1980, to design in a style that could loosely be termed "New French Classicism." It certainly refers to and takes its place within a tradition of rooms that use the French eighteenth century emphatically as a starting point but are by no means slavish recreations of that time; these are not "period" rooms. Not quite the wild eclecticism firmly rooted in Napoleon III's Second Empire or *le style Rothschild* either, it might be termed *le style Patino* after the Chilean tin-mining family whose taste in houses, beginning in the 1950's, did almost as much to promote an appreciation of the French decorative arts as the Rothschild banking dynasty had done a half-century before.

Developed in Catroux's hands after Ferrières in several houses for the Patino family in Paris, Portugal, and New York, he takes the style out of its early days—think crimson damask, Boulle furniture, and Dutch still-life paintings—and into a lighter palette of beige, white, and gray. Seventeenth- and eighteenth-century French furniture is still plentiful but paintings by Franz Hals are replaced with modern art, shapes of upholstered pieces become more contemporary, and with a more neutral architectural and chromatic backdrop *le style Patino* becomes *le style Catroux*: an expression of French style that is still grand, but thoroughly rooted in the twentieth century. Most of the projects by Catroux from the late 1970s to after 2000 are in this neo-traditional vein, but with their backdrops of whites, beiges, and café au lait they are all about Catroux's self-professed interest in lightness and whiteness. Color, however, is never fully abandoned.

PARIS, 1963

A word about influences, and another meeting that amounted to a significant event in the young life of our subject. The French decorator/architect Catroux most strongly admires is Emilio Terry, a genius of Irish and Cuban descent best known for his work for Charles de Bestegui at the Chateau de Groussay. Terry was a highly individualistic designer; unusually, his primary talent was as an architect, but he was also a very original colorist. In his work from the 1930s until his death in 1969 he investigated the potential of the baroque and neoclassical styles to be interpreted as *modern*, describing himself once with eloquence and economy as "the inventor of the Louis XVII style." The traditional French decorator to whom Catroux's work most closely relates, however, is Georges Geoffroy. Active from the 1940s until his death in 1971 and not as widely remembered today as he should be (if you ask someone in a position to know who was the greatest

François and Betty's apartment on the rue de Condé, designed in the neoclassical style that characterized the 1980's. Catroux's interest in architecture is now manifested in classical rustication, rather than the platforms and open volumes of a dozen years before. However, *le plus ça change* . . . the Atlas is still with us, the coromandel screen which had floated above their platform bed is now split on either side of the fireplace, and the medallion by Jean Dunand (it started life as a tabletop) has become an overdoor.

Gathered white drapery was a device used to decorate rooms in the classical world—it was used by Percier and Fontaine at Malmaison—but Catroux insists he was thinking of none of these, and just wanted to cover up the fussy nineteenth-century moldings on the walls. The carpet is continuous, as a real stone floor might be.

Beige but never boring. Regence, Boulle, and Louis XVI furniture, a vocabulary which uses all the opulence of eighteenth-century French decorative arts — yet a 1989 Paris apartment by Catroux still has "young energy," probably thanks to its neutral palette and a collection of superb modern art.

of the French, the most inventive—the decorator's decorator—chances are they will nod slowly at the mention of Geoffroy). In his work he managed to be both stately and highly original with interiors such as an *hôtel particulier* for Christian Dior and the private apartment of Alexis de Rede at Hotel Lambert. One of the things François Catroux is searching for in the work of this middle period is to bring to "traditional" French decorating, whether in exported form on Park or Fifth avenues or in one of the great *hôtel particuliers* of Saint Germain, in the country of its birth with proportions to soar, some of the individuality and energy he saw in the work of Georges Geoffroy. If Geoffroy's style can be explained in a sentence, one might say that whenever possible he found ways of combining grandeur with the eccentric.

Catroux became acquainted with Geoffroy in the early 1960s when he was brought to meet the older designer at his apartment on the rue de Rivoli by another decorator, Gerard Mille. What Catroux found there was different than the work of Henri Samuel, who executed grand interiors that were highly successful but also immaculate, crowd-pleasing, and known for their symmetry and decorum (only after 1970 and principally in his own apartment did Samuel begin to experiment with contemporary pieces). It was also different from the work of Emilio Terry, though Terry and Geoffroy rank as equals in the category of breaking new ground. Long before Samuel incorporated risk into his approach to design, and in similarly elegant circumstances, Geoffroy used mind-bending color combinations (the vivid, inky reds and greens of a Technicolor musical or Charles James gown) combined with the architectural restraint of Ledoux and the Directoire as a backdrop. The surprise appearance of something unexpected often came in the form of furniture by the minimalist *ébéniste* Joseph Gengenbach (known as Canabas), active in France in the very late eighteenth century but whose pieces, typically made of naked mahogany and bereft of the usual complement of ormolu mounts, seem to come from no place or time at all.

In the originality and rule-breaking of Georges Geoffroy, and in his peculiar gift for conjuring a modern feeling out of a room full of antiques, François Catroux found a road map to handling "history," and the attendant *seriousness* of French eighteenth-century tradition, with aplomb. If you seek the thread connecting the post-1980 Catroux style to that of Geoffroy from the 1950s and 60s and lose your way, look for the odd piece by Canabas—it is usually there somewhere.

The irony of being recognized by the very wealthy as a decorator of choice is that it also presents a challenge. While in one sense anything is possible, most affluent people actually want to live the way they see other affluent people living whom they admire; as the numbers go higher, there is less appetite for fantasy and experimentation. The times change too, and revolutionary moments like 1967 don't last forever, either in politics or decoration. The challenge—besides being able to change one's style at all, which many people cannot—is to remain individualistic without needing to take positions that are unnatural or extreme. Catroux has always been a decorator of his time, and the projects from this middle period (roughly 1975–2000) in which he investigates decorating in historical styles are particularly interesting, because besides being exceptionally beautiful to look at—this is the decorating by Catroux that is perhaps easiest to love—they match the success of his early career, and were received with as much acclaim despite completely changing vocabulary from radical to classic. In them, Catroux maintains his method of resolving architectural questions first and embellishing decoration on top of that. And with a few deliberate exceptions (even if one has to squint) they *are* modern—though with a sense of modernism that is arrived at by instinct, as though a sound or rhythm has perhaps been subconsciously injected between the actual notes of music. This oblique approach stands in contrast to his early work, where to be modern *was* the point.

"He has a view of things which is flexible about style, but consistent about quality."—New York client

PARIS, 2015

As you look at the work depicted in these pages, consider for a moment the size of the Atelier Catroux today: seven people plus the principal, including the office manager. Two of the interior architects have been with Catroux for forty and forty-one years respectively at the time of writing ("Interior architect" is a term which does not really exist in the United States but translates roughly to having the ability to create technical working drawings of any part of a building but its exterior). Catroux, himself an interior architect albeit without degree, recognizes the primary importance of that skill in the execution of his interiors and is quick to point out the importance of two key members of his team. For virtually their entire careers since graduating from the École Boulle, Jean-Yves Davaille and Paul Descoutures have been key employees within the office of François Catroux. With their graphic and technical skills, and most critically, their ability to intuit the intent of their employer, they are indispensable. "So good," in Catroux's own words, "that they do the work of fifteen people."

The office itself is an intimate space on two levels in the rue du Faubourg Saint-Honoré. Outfitted as a practical and utilitarian workplace, it is not itself an environment designed to be fashionable at all, though it is in a very fashionable part of town. Catroux works alone on the upper level surrounded by samples and books like a ship's captain on the bridge, phoning down constantly to the drafting room. The entire place, upstairs and down, might be 180 square meters. There is an atmosphere of respect and camaraderie—but also the peculiarly French formality and protocol surrounding a creative personality who is revered (the jeweler Joel Rosenthal, working down the street under the better-known acronym JAR, is referred to in-house as *"Le Maître"*). This is exemplified by the office manager, who despite being there nine years and knowing many intimate details of her employer's life always refers to him as "Monsieur Catroux." "I could never call him François," she explains, "or '*tutoie*' him personally." He is a firm and demanding boss—but, unusually for a decorator at the very top, not one known for his temper.

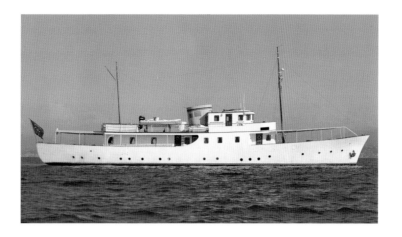

"*Deianeira* is a boat very dear to me. It's a dream boat, because the owner and I knew each other well—for fifteen years I had been invited to go sailing aboard this boat from the 1950s, which he would charter, and spend the time talking about what we would do to improve the design. One day he bought her, and I got to fix it all the things we had talked about."

Fairly obviously from these photographs, the owners of this sixteenth-century manor house "were big collectors of antiques of all kinds," recalls Catroux. "Paintings, porcelain, etc." The solution was to combine all these objects in what he describes as an "Haute Époque" style, a Renaissance collector's cabinet sympatico to the era of the architecture.

"I've never seen any of them, but my favorite thing might be his boats." — Paris client

Now consider the output of work by this small team, particularly what it takes to create the boats. The yacht *Limitless* (pp. 90–97), from first drawing to launch in 1997, took over three years. During this period the Atelier Catroux was as busy as it has ever been, which means handling an average of maybe four other active projects at the same time. Catroux and his key employees made frequent trips to the Lurssen shipyard in Bremen, Germany (the same shipbuilders as *Eos* [pp. 182–95]), coordinating their working drawings for every aspect of the interior—lamps, upholstery, carpets, furniture, paneling and millwork details—with those of the naval architecture of the boat itself. A full-size mock-up for the yacht's main stair was created in wood before the real one was built of steel. The organization required to execute this level of design and coordinate it with the architectural envelope makes the nautical projects an interesting case study in the power of output versus quantity of personnel. Aesthetically the boats also contain interesting examples of the evolution of the Catroux style: full of technical problems and limited spaces that require ingenuity and, most importantly, the power of illusion to be overcome, they invite innovation. One can see aboard *Limitless* certain finishes and details that become dress rehearsals for ideas developed fifteen years later for *Eos,* eventually making their way into terrestrial applications as well.

"I love black, beige, and white. I could do all my houses in this." — François Catroux

NEW YORK CITY, 1986

Today, committed again to decorating in a modern style, a project by François Catroux as likely as not can consist of a palette of beige and white, or blacks and grays. One of the first apartments to strike out in this more minimal direction is the pied-à-terre for an international couple at the Carlyle Hotel in New York, executed in 1986 (pp. 70–77). Here, to disguise the small scale of an apartment which, however luxurious, is still a compact hotel suite with unprepossessing ceiling heights, some interesting architectural tricks are deployed. This is primarily an apartment in the Art Deco style, but the expected crown moldings and door casings are eliminated and a substitute found in the curious architectural device of shagreen quoins (elements resembling the blocks of cut stone often found on the corners of a building's exterior) that allude to the New York skyscraper context. Just before this project Catroux also uses illusionistic cut stone (or rustication) extensively at his own apartment on the rue de Condé. It's 1983 and he's dipping his toe rather gingerly into Postmodernism, so in Paris the material represented by faux stone *is* stone (and in the spirit of the time, paired with a carpet of marbleized octagons). But in New York the quoins become faux sharkskin, a nod to both the sensuality of illusion and the precedent of frequent use of this material by Art Deco *ébénistes* like Emile-Jacques Ruhlmann and Pierre Legrain.

As with his boats, there is an undercurrent of practicality that justifies design decisions. The quoins in the Carlyle living room replace the expected traditional moldings with an irreverent aesthetic surprise. A good architect, however, never deploys tricks without a second layer of rationalization, and here in the bedroom the quoins morph into three dimensions and extrude from the wall to become built-in bedside tables. To disguise the ceiling heights, all the upholstered seating is low—we find sofas on the way to being banquettes in the tailored shapes of Milo Baughmann, and in place of the usual leggy chairs a pair of exotic African folding seats which may or may not actually be sat upon. A Botero floats over a wall of architectural mirror at the south end of the room, doubling the light and creating a layered illusion of endless space. True to Catroux's commitment to the transcendence of designing in a single period, the picture is also here to redeem the apartment from being too much of a meditation on an Art Deco theme, firmly claiming a place for it in the realm of the contemporary. No goal is more important to this designer, particularly when working with objects of exceptional value, than to stay young.

BEVERLY HILLS, 2012

The moment identifiable in the 1986 Carlyle apartment as a turning point back to modernism comes to perhaps its fullest expression in the 2012 Coldwater Canyon house in Beverly Hills (pp. 222–37), a major tour de force in the later Catroux style. The Carlyle apartment and this project form brackets to the third phase of Catroux's career in which the somewhat improbable self-expressed dream of working in an entirely neutral palette is explored, if not consistently fulfilled. In between them, on a journey which continues into the present and may be described very loosely as going from white to gray and back again—with particular commitment to exploring the possibilities of grays—there are many other beautiful and successful forays into this minimalistic world. These are the projects shown here for clients in London, Hong Kong, and Paris, as well as the three-masted sailing yacht *Eos*.

Not the least of this category is François and Betty's own apartment on the rue de Lille (pp. 160–71). This space is an intimate but very gracious ground-floor suite with two bedrooms, which Catroux has used as a sort of lab for his later design ideas. It is where many of the gestures and vocabulary later expanded upon in the Coldwater Canyon living room were first worked out: upholstery in gray and neutral tones on undulating forms by Kagan or Royere, seat furniture arrayed diagonally atop rugs of circular or organic form. It was this rue de Lille apartment, then newly redone, which I first came to visit and wrote about for the *Wall Street Journal* in the December 2011 issue of *WSJ Magazine*. Knowing best the style of Catroux's middle period, with its history of strong colors and equally strong reliance on antique furniture, I went to Paris thinking I would find something more classical ("*trés Jacob*," as he might describe it, referencing the mahogany used by the eighteenth Century *ébéniste*). It was a revelation to find his latest work in such an original and futuristic vein, full of palm wood rather than mahogany and making such an unexpected connection—perhaps it is better to describe it as a bridge—between the projects from the beginning of his career, and those of today.

"In my mind, what interests me most is architecture. It's always a question of architecture for me: proportion, volume, and very good detailing."
— François Catroux

Very much in evidence in the Coldwater Canyon house is Catroux's commitment to architecture to generate the direction of his interiors. In this project—not a new house but the comprehensive renovation of an existing Spanish-style building that stopped just short of tearing it down—he taps the potential of certain materials to suggest things about a design and endow it with a strong direction or narrative power. Two significant gestures set the course here architecturally: first is the random and irregular dark gray stone with which the interior walls are almost completely veneered—this material has a deliberately external character and leads us to believe we may be in a building by Frank Lloyd Wright or one of his disciples. Then there is the woodwork of the balcony and ceiling trusses, bulked up and ebonized to imply a structural role (though of course it has none) in the form of heavy beams and a massive cantilevered upper room. This process, a one-two punch of two big decisions to carry the room (one of field and one of line, though it's the stone that really counts here) is pure Catroux, and affirms the source of his perception of himself as an interior architect first and only after that a decorator. When he does decorate, the woods from which a pair of Nakashima chairs are constructed (American walnut and black hickory) and the familiar, innocent quality of their forms gives the living room a "regional" connection to California. This is offset by the otherworldly drama of chamois-covered pieces of upholstery by Kagan and Royere, towering lamps by Mauro Fabbro, and sculptural furniture by Wendell Castle, a 1970s/80s American designer whose revival is on the rise but whose work was a very singular choice at the time.

The design formula, if it can be decoded, goes something like this: Catroux, upon encountering the volume of the existing house, ignores the stucco and tile "existing conditions" of Southern California and perceives an empty vessel. Instead he asks himself, "What is the architecture that could take place in this space—in this region, in this climate, for these clients? Supported by an answer that generates the direction architecturally, in this case the Wright/Taliesin cue, he then asks how to fill this vessel, a question which might go along these lines: "How much imagination through décor— the layering of furniture and objects—can then be brought to bear atop this architectural point of view, and still yield a credible result?" Lastly he might wonder: "What is the role of color?" Though as we have seen, and is certainly the case in this house, lately he hasn't been worrying about that so much.

"François is very good because he has the flexibility to make a project look like the client." — South American client

In the personality of the Coldwater Canyon client, a close friend with whom he has already collaborated on two projects (the two Rue de Seine apartments in Paris from 1985 and 2004), both of which *are* very successful as portraits of their owner, there was already a design rapport. But for this client and her husband as a couple, in a house that had been *his* home since long before their marriage—he bought the property in 1975 and it was his attachment to it that led to the decision to renovate rather than start with a clean slate—something exciting and really new was required (not to mention this is Los Angeles—a town where any fantasy is possible and basically there are no rules). The answer? Power Taste but new taste, and a meditation on Frank Lloyd Wright—not literally, but as if depicted by Cedric Gibbons in a noir film set.

The interior spaces of this house are otherworldly and something truly not seen before, not just in the sense of their architecture but the contents as well. In the living room we find the surprise of enormous armchairs covered in silvery chamois (the long, trailing neck hair of Alpine rams), and in the master bath Numidian marble of pink and green, something Richard Morris Hunt might have thought about using in Newport and then lost his nerve. A tree grows through the main space, begging the very Californian question of whether we are ever actually inside. This house is in every sense a provocation and a success—both as an original aesthetic adventure into new ground, full of risk and surprises—and as a completely fresh backdrop for the life of a very singular couple at the pinnacle of the two worlds of business and design. It also manifests itself as the portrait of its owners which the wife knew would emerge (look hard enough, and you will see a portrait of its creator as well). But what no one could have guessed, and testifies to Catroux's skill at manipulating architectural challenges to advantage, was that the project would actually come out stronger because of the decision to keep and reinvent the old house rather than starting with a blank slate.

Also possessed of an exotic beauty and similarly hard to classify is the villa in Hong Kong (pp. 196–209). Not a house, conventionally speaking, but a private gallery and entertaining space for another repeat Catroux client who is also a close friend. The couple is truly an international one (these are the same owners of the apartment at the Carlyle Hotel), but their business is based in Hong Kong. Besides being voracious and encyclopedic collectors they are also quite adventurous in their personal taste ("daring," as Catroux describes it).

This compact Palladian villa in a dramatic and isolated setting high on Victoria Peak contains relatively few but grandly proportioned rooms. The design is organized for the owners to use the more intimately scaled lower level as personal space, and the main floor for entertaining only and as a sort of private museum. This is another unique environment by Catroux, and along with the Coldwater Canyon house it is the recent work he is most proud of. It's also a little hard to understand—strange, and so striking as to be somewhat eerie—until he explains the motivation behind the design. "Being in Hong Kong, the easy and expected way would have been to do the house in a sort of British colonial style. Instead I suggested we use lots of pieces by Claude Lalanne, with bronze gingko leaves—things like crocodile benches, etc., to bring the tropical atmosphere from the jungle surroundings *inside*."

Luxury comes in many forms. There's the luxury of comfort, the luxury of convenience, the luxury of opulence. In this house the primary definition of luxury seems to be in the abandonment of convention—it doesn't have to function as a conventional house, remember, but to dazzle at night—and in the "daring" of the clients' taste. Luxury here comes in the expression that ultimately on this site, for these clients, anything is possible—any collection, any combination of objects and architecture, any rejection of convention can be indulged. It is a very sophisticated interpretation of luxury to choose narrow casement windows to frame such a view, and to turn a white Palladian box into a container for a Golden Ribbon light fixture by Ingo Maurer and paintings by Damien Hirst. The luxury here comes from contrast in all forms and in particular from sensual experience, of hearing the squeak of old parquet as you confront a neon work by Joseph Kosuth.

The villa contains many smaller surprises. It is a thoroughly classical building, newly constructed but designed deliberately as a foil for exclusively modern art. The tone of its contents is set by one of the most extensive collections, if not the most, of Lalanne furniture in an environment which is basically defined by it. In the large drawing room the suite of Louis XV giltwood armchairs is covered in Kandinsky-inspired Pierre Frey fabric, embroidered by Lesage with a Chinese geometric pattern chosen by Catroux. Embroidery and texture are a theme here. Turn a corner and find Gaetano Pesce's "Up" chair with its tethered ball ottoman, a playful Pop upstart among the stark white classical detailing and ebonized *parquet de Versailles* floors. The monumental tufted double-sided sofa in the main space has crocodiles' feet of gilded wood designed to relate to the menagerie of Lalanne furniture. They look inevitable now, next to all the other crocodiles and having listened to Catroux's explanation of his intent to refer to the jungle—like psychedelic William Kent. But besides showing the care and imagination that goes into a unique project like this, the feet also provide a window into all the hard work that is an essential part of the process. To this day, several years after completion, the discarded trial models of other creatures' feet and paws in wood and resin—lions mostly, but also birds and maybe a bear—are still in Catroux's office.

So how does this story end? The simple answer is that it does not. It does not end because Catroux shows no interest in slowing down, in reducing his workload or travel schedule, or in contemplating retirement. His office is flourishing and he recently finished two projects in California that required traveling there from Paris every month. He has just begun projects in Saudi Arabia and New York City which are among the largest of his career. Besides this continuing activity and relevance, another incentive that led me to pursue the story of his life in design were all the threads I kept encountering, scattered over decades in the form of magazine stories and images in books. What did they add up to? Who was this designer, really—and with such a diversified body of work, what did he stand for? How could one person have been capable of being the best modernist—and then the best historicist—and then the best modernist again? Lastly, why—after so much time and so many triumphs—was there no book on what amounted to *the* great untold story in the history of interior design? And why didn't he seem to care about that?

The simple answer is he was busy. Because like many of the best decorators—in particular Catroux's early touchstone Billy Baldwin—in his work François Catroux seems to be getting younger with age. However, after a career spanning nearly fifty years, it's time to talk about the delicate subject of legacy. Indulging in generalizations can be perilous, but it seems fair to say that a significant part of the cultural identity of France is derived from a tradition of excellence in three fields: fashion, cuisine, and the decorative arts. This last is now a term interchangeable with interior design, and who you ask determines the order of importance—but a chef, a decorator, or a fashion designer will all tell you that the French consider their superiority in these areas to be a sacred national tradition.

More than a matter of talent and accomplishment among individuals, achievements in these arts form a contribution to a cultural legacy that is linear and ongoing. It can also be said that talent at the top is thought of as something transferred between generations like a baton, as happened between Christian Dior and Yves Saint Laurent, or inherited (though perhaps not so much by the principals, who love to claim no influences or may admit to at most one, usually Marie-Laure de Noailles). Bigger than any single person or career, being one of the great decorators of France has a different significance of meaning than in England or Italy, for instance, where that stature might instead be conferred upon a Shakespearian actor, opera singer, or comedian. In France decoration at the highest level is part of a national tradition, a torch to be passed.

Since the death of Yves Saint Laurent in 2008 the question of who can fill his shoes in the world of fashion is still being debated. Following the death of Henri Samuel in 1996, a similar question arose as to who would carry on the legacy of interior design as a mode of national artistic expression. Scaling the heights of the French design world today, compared to past decades the early aughts by no means present themselves as a golden age. But François Catroux is at the top, presiding serenely as a decorator who values comfort over mischief. His background and his nature have made him a forward-thinker who is decidedly anti-nostalgic, but not exactly in favor of revolution either; he is never a proponent of the New merely for newness's sake. As a designer Catroux also has a very humanistic outlook, and something "new" must also be an agreeable experience for the clients (his user-friendly approach comes through clearly in Diane's foreword to this book). Catroux is a decorator who puts a high value on elegance and understatement, always in response to architecture first, and eschews the zaniness of trends. He is unafraid of risks as we have seen, but is also a decorator who believes that style should be measured not merely in risks taken, but in successes gained.

The mission of assembling the images in this book is to show in its entirety for the first time the fifty-year narrative of Catroux's career. In telling his story, it is also to place that career contextually in the history of twentieth-century design, and to make clear that despite the diversity of styles in which he has worked he is no less a champion of a French point of view in decoration than any of his peers, present or past. Like Emilio Terry's neat characterization of his own work as having added the "unfinished" chapters to the Louis XVI style, François Catroux has given new form to the French interior design canon. Catroux began as an innovator; in his work he has done that consistently, if not exclusively (there are the "steel fireplace" moments of striking originality, and there are also the less-easy-to-identify—but just as important—moments of subtle innovation such as the reinvention of nineteenth-century upholstered forms into what amounts to contemporary furniture in the 1990 Park Avenue apartment in New York [pp. 78–89]). But even when he has not broken new ground, instead opting to work with subtle gestures in an existing language—as when, building upon the example of Georges Geoffroy, he exchanges the regal colors typical of traditional French rooms for a palette of browns and creams to make the eighteenth century seem fresh again—once understood they are clear evidence of genius.

Can *you* think of another room anywhere like the Coldwater Canyon living room in Los Angeles? The only design precedent might be the house belonging to James Mason's villainous character near Mount Rushmore in *North by Northwest*—and that was a dream, a fiction, a concoction of matte painting and movie set by Alfred Hitchcock. We know Catroux's stone interior of the Coldwater house explicitly references Frank Lloyd Wright, though perhaps in the context of Hollywood it also does contain a reference to Hitchcock. But whatever the source, the "mission accomplished" here is the conjuring of a connection to the narrative of American modernism from a very unexpected and specific moment with the economy of a single gesture—one rugged architectural material—which bestows on the house a sense of "place." This room is a radical, original event, and it was executed when Catroux was in his mid-70s, what many people in his position would have considered an attractive time to be contemplating retirement.

To paraphrase the client who has collaborated with Catroux on some of the most ravishing design history depicted here who put the question so eloquently at the start: you may decide to call him a European decorator, or a French decorator. But there can be no doubt that in accumulating this body of work over the last five decades—quietly, relentlessly, and brilliantly, as Yves Saint Laurent and Paul Bocuse did in their fields and Henri Samuel and Emilio Terry once did in his—that François Catroux has lifted the field of design, serially and with complete personal authorship, across at least three different eras. And through the remarkable career depicted in these pages he has done what only happens once or twice in a generation in any field: he has enabled France, in one of its most cherished national art forms, to come into the fullness of its inheritance.

"My apartment on Quai de Béthune happened during the French revolutionary year of 1968, when everyone was *against* everything—and without knowing it myself, I was against everything too. Against *things*, so for two years I thought only of volumes and levels, without any furniture . . . cushions instead of a sofa, a cube for a coffee table . . . "

"No commodes, no settees. Only volumes, and art."

"It's like a bed which is like a house which is inside the room. A new version for 1968 —*my* version—of an eighteenth-century four-poster bed. I was the first person to do something like this, which for me is more important than the steel mantels."

"Maybe I was influenced by David Hicks
when I chose that rug, I don't remember.
But I found the African sculpture,
and I still love that painting by Helen
Frankenthaler. The room had a superb
Ellsworth Kelly we don't see."

"My first project in New York City was also the first time I worked with such important art. It was very difficult to work with Paul Rudolph, who was the architect, hating the decorator as every architect does . . . "

"Paul Rudolph did the shape of the bookcase, and I did the leather inside, the fur rug, and all that."

"The son of the owners was helping with the paintings. It was he who found the Twombly in the living room, and also the James Rosenquist in the library [p. 48]."

"Olympic Tower was a very fashionable building for the Europeans in New York. I did three apartments there. This was the first one, and I can remember going up when the building was not finished on an outside elevator with Onassis, who was the builder, Hélène Rochas, and the couple whose apartment is pictured here . . . Forty-five stories high in the wind, it was a disaster."

"I loved the large-scale *poche* print of this velvet at that time. Like Fortuny—but it was American, I think. Maybe Larsen. The scale of the print was eighteenth-century, but the material was very modern. So I think it went very well with the old furniture of these clients."

"I chose much of the furniture myself from their collection, but the desk we bought at Mallett. So we went to London, shopping for a French apartment in New York."

"This is a very important apartment for me, because I was given carte blanche and I couldn't blame anybody but myself if it wasn't a big success. The client was an American banker living in Paris, and he said 'I want you to do something *sparkling.*' That was it, all the direction I received."

"The bedroom was great, and the bathroom in the same style just behind the screen of ebonized wood. You find the same work and detail in *Eos* [pp. 182–95], inspired by Japanese documents from the eighteenth century which are so *modern*. I love this style and I come back to it again and again."

"This is a project of mine I like very much, because it's from a show at the Grand Palais that only existed for three weeks but has been copied in every hotel in the world. The same stone, but sometimes honed and sometimes polished, the very shallow sink carved from a single large piece."

"These sconces were made by me, but I must say I got the inspiration
from a brasserie in downtown New York. A huge place from the 1930s,
full of columns inside, and on top of each column were four of these."

"One day, the CEO of the French national high-speed railway came to see me. They wanted a train in very high style to go between Paris and Strasbourg. So I did the project, the train was in operation for one year, and then poof— it stopped. But not because of *me*."

"Joël Robuchon was the chef. There were no meetings between him and myself, and I never got to travel on it, but I did go two or three times to the factory near Lille where the cars were produced. Some cars were upholstered in gray and yellow, some orange and brown as these pictures show."

"I'm always trying to make the apartments I'm doing in accordance with the country or city where they are. The Carlyle is a very New York building, so this apartment is a mixture of Art Deco from that, but also African and Asian (the Noguchi paper lights everywhere, because the couple lives in Hong Kong)."

"A lot of Art Deco designers were influenced by Africa. This apartment has both the source and its progeny, real African furniture and interpretations of the French *moderne* style."

"The rooster is by François Pompon, who was the Lalanne of the nineteenth century. He did lots of animals."

"Rustication is here to bring this sense of the building's architecture inside the apartment, instead of on the outside where it really exists. And to make them more refined, the blocks were painted in faux shagreen."

"The collection of this family is enormous. Of course I did what everybody else would have done, which is to organize it, and group in each room a different period of painting."

"All the Dutch paintings are what inspired the decoration in the dining room—also a seventeenth-century cabinet inlaid with ebony, ivory, and tortoiseshell. The whole room is faux-painted in a scheme that sprang from that cabinet, and even the tiles around the fireplace are painted, not real."

"I prefer this building to my other apartment house in New York. It's a great building by Rosario Candela. The architecture remained the same—the layout, I mean, and the shape of the rooms—but I created the architectural details. Pediments, architraves, all new but looking like they belong there."

"One of the things I like about this apartment is the distribution of the rooms, that you can always see from one room to another. Especially from the library. This is the sort of classical style I like for New York—not French paneling, Louis XV. I mean, the Mayflower was bringing Dutch, English, and Irish people to America. No French."

"Many of the painted architectural details on the walls and the rug come from the ceiling. I think of the upholstery as modern—I wasn't thinking of a nineteenth-century *bourne* at the time, but I wanted to do something more interesting than a pair of sofas or back-to-back sofas. So it is a new version of something that in the nineteenth century would have been deeply tufted, but still with the fringe."

"Maybe the Magritte is my favorite painting in this room. But the Modigliani is a very good one, too."

"The first boat I ever did was called was called *Sayonara* for Hélène Rochas, but the *Limitless* was my first *big* boat. In this sort of work they give you the empty hull. Jon Bannenberg did a beautiful design for the boat. I loved working for this client— our ideas always corresponded, and I did twelve planes for him, department stores . . . Each thing I've done for him was a success, because of him as much as me."

"The thing that makes this boat really extraordinary is the amount of open outdoor decks. Not much superstructure for a megayacht."

"There are only five cabins, also unusual for a boat this size."

"I try to make corners of intimacy in the big salons. This owner is a fantastic client, and a very *rare* client. He has a goal, he is focused, and when we discuss a project he has the attention to remain completely involved in all details until the very end."

"This client is a frustrated decorator, to start with. The way he has always worked with me, for over a decade, is to arrive in my office to discuss the plan—then take up a piece of tracing paper and try to do better than me. Changing, moving a wall . . . but in the end, always saying 'you are right!'"

"Framed on the walls are pages from a fabulous book of maritime drawings from 1768 by Frederik Henrik af Chapman, *Architectura Navalis Mercatori*. We covered the whole boat with these."

"This salon is a huge room, and it humanizes the scale to have the white planks on the ceiling. Which I did on *Eos* [pp. 182–95], too."

"Ah, my house in the country, in Lourmarin. What can I say, of course I love it. This is *my* house. I bought a ruin, and this is why I bought it, *because* it was a ruin. So there was nothing to destroy, it was already terrible — but I loved the location, and I especially loved the vaults on the ground floor."

"*Les Ramades* is a sixteenth-century building. It's not a farm, not a manor . . . Some people told me it was once a convent, and somebody else told me it was the house of important people who lived in the village in the sixteenth and seventeenth centuries."

"The design of this floor is called a *calade*, when you press all the stones into cement close together. It's not an original idea—you see it in many houses in the south of France. But I wanted the design because it gives the cracks a place to happen in a line where the pebbles are, instead of in the middle. If you squint, it's like a Moroccan rug that travels throughout the house."

"I bought the house for the vaults."

"This was supposed to be our room. But then when it was all finished, we decided that the best room for us was a tiny room overlooking the garden. This became the VIP guest room all our friends love to stay in, and I still have never spent the night here. The frieze is a line from the *Fables* of La Fontaine, and do you know where that round mirror is from? Crate & Barrel, bought in Los Angeles. I don't hesitate to mix."

"We are not often in this room because the idea is to always be outside. But fortunately this is the room you have to pass through to *get* outside, so we see it every day. It's more like a gallery than a dining room, but it's not a dead room."

"Al fresco for drinks. Off this terrace is
the little room Betty and I chose to sleep
in, straight ahead with the shutters open.
It's like sleeping *in* the garden."

"Betty is not attached to houses at all, she doesn't care. She swims and she drinks. The rest of the house and the garden is me—and she likes it that way. But if anything is wrong, she notices immediately. The mirrors are made from wheels of agricultural machinery I bought at the Isle-sur-la-Sorgue flea market."

"There were big wars in this area in the
sixteenth century between Protestants and
Catholics and all the houses were fortified,
which is why we have the courtyard."

"This is a landmark building in Paris,
an eighteenth-century *hôtel particulier*.
I wanted to return it to the spirit of
the original architecture, and to work
in a building like this you have to ask
permission from the *bureau des monuments
historiques*. I had to fight with them because
everything existing was in fact from the
nineteenth century, to prove that our
designs resembled what originally had
been. I transformed the inside completely
to return to the purity of the original style.
All the architecture you see is new."

"So for me, and I hope it's not too pretentious, I think it's a great interpretation of the eighteenth century in a modern way. In a *today* way."

"I have a series of document books of architectural elements by an architect named Cases at the office that inspire many of the details in my work. The white and mahogany doors in the salon come from that. And the bookcases in the library that have the structure and feeling of stone, but they are faux stone."

MATHEMATICA

SCIENTIAE NATURALIS

"This library is a very masculine room, but the owner is a lady and she loves it. She really *lives* in this room."

"The little curved staircase is new. It was very difficult to make because of the headroom and issues like that, but it looks like it had always existed."

"In contrast to the library, the dining room is a very feminine room. The term for those curtains is *gigot*, and you can do that with only one fabric—it has to be taffeta, to hold the bouffant shape."

"The dining room was the missing important room we had to 'invent' for the house. The original ceiling was much lower, at the height of the windows, which actually stop below the arches. We added those arches when we raised it, which have no glass, and then mirrored them on the other side containing illuminated shelves. The trellis is the grille for the air conditioning."

"Chanel and the Duke of Westminster were the first tenants of this apartment, and it was she who commissioned the ceiling paintings from José Maria Sert, which were completely concealed when we started."

"The big *horloge* was the first thing I placed in this hallway, an incredible calendar/clock which came from Didier Aaron and has a case probably by Canabas. You can see it in this client's first apartment on page 24."

"I bought the Boulle desk, but the concept of this room is really to group all the black and white works of art together."

"The most important object of them all is the sixteenth-century Augsburg atlas in vermeil, which ranks alongside the Giacometti [see p. 145]. There are many treasures here, but the main idea to bring unity and lightness to the apartment—which is just as important— was to make all the rugs in straw. It would have been too heavy, with so many objects of this value, to have antique carpets as well."

"This apartment is one of my favorite of all the 'antique' things I have done. In the library we started with the Empire chandelier. So we decided to use the Empire style for the bookcases as well, and the cornice and the rest of the architecture follows in that 'end of the eighteenth, beginning of the nineteenth century' style."

"The incredible Léger, from the 1910s and maybe one of the best in the world, belonged to the client's father."

"The library is the only room where we didn't use a plain straw rug, but an antique needlepoint one over the straw. That leather bed I made for the apartment before, to go in a niche. The Picasso is from the late 1940s, one of his Louisette portraits."

"The chandelier and sconces were commissioned for the room by Lalanne, original Louis XV paneling, and the fantastic chairs are *regence*, a splendid model. The clients are extremely chic and refined and they eat on the bronze silk damask, really using it. So I made about twelve tablecloths like this of damask."

149

"This one is a good mixture of my *rigueur* and the fantasy of this client who is my good friend. It's the second apartment we have done together on the rue de Seine in Paris. When I finished, everything was bare—chocolate, white, and beige—very strict, like I like to do—and she said 'I can't live like this,' and added the color. Any time you see strong color like those African beaded chairs in the living room, it's her."

"These iron consoles were a gift from me . . . I bought them for myself at Lourmarin, and then I thought they were too chichi for Lourmarin but right for her apartment. And she loved them."

"Everything from the old apartment we reused, so there are ghosts of it here. That massive Charles X desk was in the library, the extraordinary plaster chair by Marina Karella in the living room . . . but the two apartments are completely different."

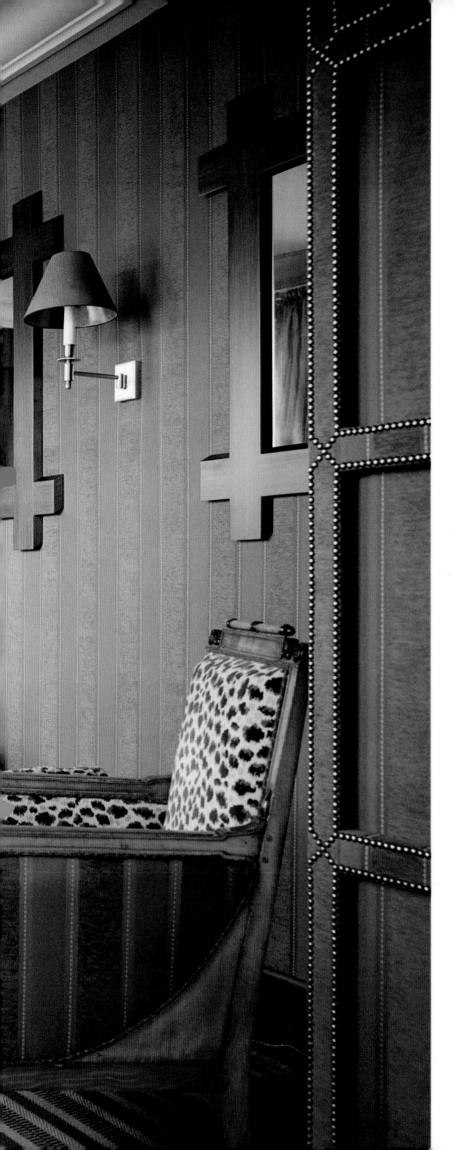

"The three mirrors in the guest room I made,
to echo the three windows on the opposite wall
overlooking the Seine and double the view."

"Welcome home. Betty loves our apartment on the rue de Lille and will never move."

"The big picture of Betty is a photo by
Phillip de Lustrac which I cut into tiles.
The Dunand table has always been with me,
but it changes—it was a table when I bought
it in 1967, then I hung it above my fireplace
like a painting on the Quai de Béthune,
and now it's a table again."

"I have many pieces by Ron Arad—more than I can use, and many things in storage. The painting is by Tom Wesselmann, and no, it's not a portrait of Betty. What I really love are these lamps by Mauro Fabbro, which I have to stop buying because they are in every picture of my work."

"The atlas was given to me as a present by Hélène Rochas. She was an intimate friend of mine, she bought a boat, and she asked me to do the decoration on the boat. I did the decoration but I didn't want to charge her anything, since I spent so much time as a guest in her beautiful houses . . . so she sent me this from Kugel. And the little Warhol portrait of Yves is from Pierre Bergé. He gave it to Betty when Yves died."

"That Arbus desk is a very important piece—historic. Bought at auction. The Starck ghost chair I like because you can mix it with everything. This is the room we really *live* in, because of the television and the books. But I hope when I add bookcases to the living room we will go in there more."

"I've got two cats, their names are Mic and Mac, and sometimes I think I am living in *their* apartment. This is Mic. I flew to Tulsa, Oklahoma, to meet the breeder and pick up one cat, and she came to the airport with *two* cats from the same parents—because they were getting along so well together she didn't want to separate them. So of course I was not going to be the one to do that, and came back to Paris with both of them."

"I love London. If I *had* to leave Paris I would go to London, which I find highly civilized. The floor of this early-eighteenth-century house on Cheyne Walk was landmarked, and I did the carpet to match the floor. Unusually for London, this house is very wide—you don't often find a salon six windows across."

"I tried everything I could to make the client buy the settee that went with the two incredible black German nineteenth-century chairs—it was a set of three. Half of the husband's family is German, so I thought it was important for them to have a piece of German 'reminiscence' in the house."

"Lalanne chandelier, Greek chairs—my carpet and my table. Any architecture can become modern if it's white, and you put the right things next to it."

"Big, generous rooms with an elegant plainness and strong contemporary art. Besides German blood, the family is mainly Greek, thus those Klismos chairs."

"Round table by Hervé Van der Straeten, whose work I love. I design these 'ribbon' carpets freehand on a piece of tracing paper. But also there is one English thing, the Regency mirror, to remind us we are near Turner's studio."

"*Eos* is the biggest sailboat in the world, ninety-six meters long, and it has made these clients happier than anything they've ever owned. When you design something like this you are never alone. The boat was built by Lurssen in Germany, the architect was Bill Langan, and the outdoor deck furnishings were by my friend Ed Tuttle who managed to make them blend beautifully with the inside."

"In the salon, we made a huge area rug precisely to fit the space, like a piece of a puzzle. I wanted it to be continuous and simple, but also to add something to the architecture and interact with it. The rug sits flush with the wood deck, so this was not easy."

"The columns are invented by me and not structural to the boat, I thought of them as a way to divide the room and make the salon more intimate."

"Down are the guest cabins, ahead to the library, and up this staircase to the owner's cabin and the wheelhouse on the upper deck. *Eos* is a modern boat, but those white boards make you feel a connection to great sailboats of the past like the *Creole*."

"This table lifts up to become a dining table, and at the touch of a button, the sofas move in to meet it. But only in case of bad weather—otherwise lunch is always on deck."

"Some of the cabins are macassar, some are mahogany. The master cabin is in sycamore and bamboo. On a boat where you use so many woods, I had to find a new idea for this guest cabin, and palm wood is exotic—one of the materials used by my favorite designers in the Art Deco style."

"The way this boat is run is fantastic, one of the best I've seen in the world. Four girls serving breakfast, but you can do what you want all day. At 6:30 every evening candles are lit in every space."

"When I got to the house it was built but empty, with only the big suspended pieces by Ingo Maurer which I adore, the disc and the ribbon. The direction of doing one big piece of furniture per room came from that starting point, to leave enough air around those works of art. The architecture is not really Palladio but English Palladianism, the revival. It looked like the house of the governor of Hong Kong to me, in a colonial way."

"The owner had collected an incredible suite of Russian eighteenth-century sconces that I used all over this main floor. The Lalanne furniture and *torchéres* we commissioned for this house are the modern counterpoint to those, to create a *galerie des glaces* as the next page really shows. I wanted to keep some of the poetry of that emptiness."

"Claude Lalanne had never done crocodile benches as big as these. She said 'Two are never going to hold, I have to add a crocodile in the middle.' I said 'In case it doesn't bend, let's have it be able to *escape* out into the room.' The benches didn't bend, and so there is that third crocodile out in front on the floor, crawling away."

"Chinese shutters in the woodwork style I love, finally *in* China. And gingko leaves to remind you that even with all the *parquet de Versailles*, we are in a tropical jungle."

"I put my own Ron Arad desk and 'Big Easy' chair in this Artcurial exhibition, which obviously relates to the new style of my apartment on rue de Lille."

"Those andirons are Mallet-Stevens, for sale with a dealer who lent them to me for the exhibition. I wish I had them now."

"A very young collector couple in London with bold taste in contemporary art. Maybe the 'blackest and whitest' of my houses like that."

"The art is the star here, like this painting by Tang Zhigang. But breaking up the furniture shapes into dark and light colors is better than all white because it looks like there's less of it."

"This apartment is my way of making an eighteenth-century landmark building in Paris, with *boiserie* and things which are very French and very *period*, into an apartment of today for a young couple."

"I think the objects I like best are the four white columns, which are not the usual height of side tables you see holding lamps next to a sofa because the ceilings here are very high. They were made for an orangerie as plant stands. Eighteenth century, same as the console. And same as the architecture."

"I was reading a book about Frank Lloyd Wright, and from that came my idea for this house. And the really Californian idea, for me, is the stone. We kept the shape of the house but changed *everything*."

"The balustrade at the mezzanine is very much inspired by Wright, and I tried to use furniture by American designers like Nakashima, Wendell Castle, and Robsjohn Gibbings—who did the "Mesa" table—with the *shapes* I love by Kagan and Royere."

"The tree had windows around it but with little divided glass. It was growing and touching the house, so we had to do something. My idea was to have the tree really *participating* with the inside of the room, to invite it inside."

"I love to shop in LA, and that table in front that looks like stones came from Blackman Cruz on La Brea. The coffee table came from auction, and I found that big Gursky photo in Hong Kong."

"The owners of this house each have a collection of nineteenth-century romantic paintings from their other houses, which I would not necessarily have chosen for this one. But the strong personality of the client, and my good friend, is in the mix."

"I was thinking of the bathroom from 1986 from the Paris exhibition [pp. 62–65] when I designed this one. Similar combination of rough and polished marble, the shallow sinks . . . "

"The spa is a separate building, away from
the house by the pool, but because you see
the stone walls again and that sofa it feels like
it belongs strongly with the house. The round
mirror turns into a television."

"The tiger is from the client's collection, the Frank Lloyd Wright chairs are me—in a house for extraordinary people who really live all over the world. But since we did this project, perhaps they think of home now as mainly LA."

I would like firstly to express my thanks to all those—most of whom have become friends—who have trusted in me to decorate their homes.

Immense thanks and gratitude go to my assistants Paul Descoutures and Jean-Yves Davaille who have worked unfailingly with me on all my projects for over 40 years.

Thanks to all the interior design journalists and magazines for featuring articles on my work throughout my career.

Special thanks to François Halard, whose photographs are largely featured in this book, as well as all the other photographers for their participation.

And finally a big thank you to David Netto for his perseverance in convincing me at last to publish this book and for the brilliant way in which he has evoked the different influences which have shaped my work.

Final thanks go to my publisher Rizzoli, in particular Douglas Curran, and the very talented Takaaki Matsumoto and his team for the elegant layout of this book.

ACKNOWLEDGMENTS

239

First published in the United States of America in 2016 by
RIZZOLI INTERNATIONAL PUBLICATIONS, INC.
300 Park Avenue South, New York, NY 10010
www.rizzoliusa.com

ISBN-13: 978-0-8478-4867-6
Library of Congress Control Number: 2016938628

Distributed to the U.S. Trade by Random House, New York

Design: Takaaki Matsumoto, Matsumoto Incorporated, New York
Design Assistant: Robin Brunelle, Matsumoto Incorporated, New York
Publication Manager: Amy Wilkins, Matsumoto Incorporated, New York

Front cover: 2009 House, Hong Kong
Back cover: 2002 Apartment, Paris

Printed and bound in China

2016 2017 2018 2019 2020 / 10 9 8 7 6 5 4 3 2 1

Photo credits
Cover: © Marianne Haas. Back cover, endpapers (front and back): © François Halard.
2, 6: © François Halard. 9: clockwise, from upper left: FC and Betty, © Jean Jacques
Bugat; FC and friend, Courtesy François Catroux; group of 4, photo by Mary Russell;
Betty and FC from *WSJ Magazine*/François Halard; group at table, photo © Jack
Nisberg/Roger-Viollet; photo of Betty and FC, photo © Horst P. Horst/Conde Nast
Collection/Getty Images; photo of FC and DVF, courtesy François Catroux; Betty and
FC by pool, courtesy François Catroux; group of 3, photo by François Catroux; photo
at center, FC, courtesy François Catroux. 15: *L'Oeil* magazine, January 1968; photos of
cover and magazine spreads by Takaaki Matsumoto; original photography © Carol-
Marc Lavrillier. 16: Décoration, photos of cover and spread by Takaaki Matsumoto;
original photography © Roger Guillemot (for *Connaissances des Arts*). 19: Photos of
magazine cover and spreads by Takaaki Matsumoto; original photography © Roger
Guillemot (for *Connaissances des Arts*). 20: Photos of magazine covers and spreads by
Takaaki Matsumoto; original interior photography © Pascal Hinous (for *Architectural
Digest*). 22: Photos of magazine covers and spreads by Takaaki Matsumoto; original
interior photography © Daniel Aron / Christian Gervais (for *Maison Française*).
23: Photos of magazine covers and spreads by Takaaki Matsumoto; original interior
photography © Michael Boys (for *House & Garden*). 24: Photos of magazine covers
and spreads by Takaaki Matsumoto; original interior photography © Jaques Dirand
(for *House & Garden*). 27: Photos © C. Coiron. 28: Photos of magazine covers and
spreads by Takaaki Matsumoto; original interior photography © Pascal Hinous (for
Architectural Digest). 39–47: © Brigitte Baert for Alberto Pinto. 47–51: © Horst P. Horst
(for Conde Nast). 53–57: Courtesy office of François Catroux. 59: © Roger Guillemot
(for *Connaissances des Arts*). 63–65: © Pascal Hinous. 67–89: © François Halard. 91–97:
© Fritz von de Shulenburg. 99–181: © François Halard. 183: © Lurssen. 184–194: ©
François Halard. 197–209: © Marianne Hass. 211–213: © Luxproduction.com. 215–217:
© Douglas Friedman. 219-221: © François Catroux. 223–238: © François Halard.